D1194228

Personnel Policies and Procedures for Nonprofit Organizations

Personnel Policies and Procedures for Nonprofit Organizations

Michael Burns & Jeremy Landau

D.A.T.A.

Development & Technical Assistance Center, Inc.

Hartford & New Haven, Connecticut

Printed in the United States of America by
Thomson-Shore, Inc., Dexter, Michigan

Design: James J. Johnson
Editing: Caroline Murphy
Production: Laura Margolin
Researcher: Eva Eszterhai

Contents

Preface   vii

Consultants Availability   xi

1.   Introduction   1

2.   Equal Employment Opportunity   6

3.   Sexual Harassment   9

4.   Job Descriptions   11

5.   Hiring of New Employees   13

6.   Job Classifications, Scheduling & Salaries   16

7.   Performance Appraisal   23

8.   Disciplinary Action   27

9.   Benefits Administration   31

10. Attendance, Vacations, Leaves of Absence   34

11. Expense Reimbursement   42

12. Termination of Employment   48

13. Privacy Code   52

14. Workplace Health and Safety   55

15. Substance Abuse   60

16. Conflicts of Interest   62

17. Posting of Notices   64

18. Signature Page   66

     Appendix 1   68

     Appendix 2   70

     Appendix 3   72

Preface

This guide is written with the belief that the more complete the personnel policies of an organization, the better prepared the nonprofit board and staff will be to manage and respond to the needs of the organization's employees and constituents. Where blanks are provided or the word 'organization' is in parentheses, feel free to add your own organization's name. In cases where blanks appear in the text, fill in these spaces with the appropriate name, title or information as it applies to your organization.

How is this guide organized?

This guide covers various employment issues for which an organization should have a general policy and, in some cases, more specific procedures. For each issue, there is a brief discussion about the purpose of the policy, a list of some of the laws or legal issues which may be pertinent to the topic, a sample policy (or policies) and, in some cases, sample procedures. The sample policies are only suggestions, and may be modified to meet the specific needs of each organization.

Who should use this guide?

This guide is designed to be used by the person or committee responsible for drafting the organization's personnel policies and manuals. This guide should not be distributed to employees as a personnel manual. It contains discussions which are meant to provide guidance in drafting a policy manual, but which are inappropriate for inclusion in the manual itself.

Personnel policies are the responsibility of an organization's board. Because policies define standards and may affect costs, the organization's owners (the board) must go through the process of developing, reviewing and acting on these guidelines. Although the responsibility for approving personnel policies rests with the board, the process of developing, encouraging, endorsing, and complying with policies may involve both management and staff.

There are several ways to involve employees in the process. Employee suggestions might be solicited and incorporated into policy statements, which then could be submitted to the employees for additional comments before the board votes on adoption. Another way would be to include staff members as part of a board committee which develops organization policies. The amount of employee input will depend on the nature of the policy, the legal restrictions, and the goals and desires of the organization itself.

Should an attorney be involved?

An attorney (preferably a volunteer, from a cost management perspective) familiar with labor and employment law should be consulted following the first draft of a set of policies. The commentary in this guide regarding laws and legal issues is designed to provide some guidance to you, but it is not all-inclusive. Appendix 1 and 2 provide additional information for identifying laws and federal regulatory agencies which may have an impact for developing personnel policies. An attorney will be able to advise you as to whether a particular state or federal law applies to your organization, and can make suggestions as to language and other choices regarding the actual policies which you adopt.

Personnel policies versus procedures

Policies are governing principles which enable decision making. Procedures are established ways for personnel to conduct themselves. Policies are the rationale for actions and may dictate consequences for not following procedures. Procedures may be included in a personnel policy handbook. Where possible, the personnel manual should distinguish between policies and procedures.

What do personnel policies achieve?

Personnel policies ensure that an organization's personnel, board and management know and understand the expectations, rights, and rules of employment by the organization. Personnel policies define the employment relationship. They establish parameters which reduce the bias, inequity, and unfairness which can occur as part of the dynamic between related and unrelated people whose cultural, educational and socio-economic backgrounds may limit their ability to address those with different backgrounds and experiences.

When should personnel policies be developed for an organization?

Ideally, policies should be developed before the first paid staff is hired. Practically, most policies will be developed when an organization has reached the stage of maturity where board roles and responsibilities are distinguished from staff roles and responsibilities. This may not occur for many years following an organization's beginning.

Many nonprofit organizations rely heavily on volunteers. Volunteers are unpaid staff. Because of the unique position of volunteers, personnel policies should be developed specifically to address volunteer management needs.

Do personnel policies constitute employment contracts?

Employment contracts define the relationship between an individual employee and an organization. Employment contracts are legal agreements which define performance expectations and the terms and conditions of employment. Personnel policies describe the nature of the employment place and the general rules of behavior. They are guidelines, not employment contracts. Note, however, that courts in several states have found that personnel manuals or policy statements may form the basis for employment contracts. For this reason, each manual should contain a disclaimer which states that the manual provides only policies and guidelines and does not constitute an employment contract. To make it easier for you to track your organization's policies, Appendix 3, a sample employee personnel record, has been provided for your use, and can be copied for each employee.

Acknowledgments

Mike Burns and Jeremy Landau wish to express their gratitude to the law firm of Robinson and Cole of Hartford, Connecticut for their commitment to the nonprofit sector and understanding of the importance of well-developed personnel policies. In particular, we would like to thank attorneys Jean Tomasco and Alice DeTora whose expertise and knowledge give this guide credibility.

Consultant Availability

Staff Development

This guide is adaptable to a variety of purposes. It is laid out so that agency staff and board members may use it as it is relevant to their agency.

However, the authors are available for individual consultation and training in order to better assist agency staff and board members in applying these broad principles to agency management.

Agency Development

This guide may be adapted to fit the specific needs of a variety of agencies and organizations. Consultations may be arranged directly with the authors to develop a personnel handbook that is an agency-specific document.

For further information, please contact:

Michael Burns, Executive Director
D.A.T.A, Inc.
70 Audubon Street
New Haven, Connecticut 06510
1–800–788–5598

Jeremy Landau, Executive Director
National AIDS Support Center
1915 Rosina
Santa Fe, New Mexico 87501
505–986–8337

1

Introduction

Discussion

Once your organization has adopted personnel policies and procedures, you may choose to include them in a manual for distribution to employees. You may choose to have additional policies for supervisors and therefore may need two policy manuals. The manual should contain an introduction which explains the purpose of the manual, names the persons responsible for amending and interpreting the manual, and includes a disclaimer that the manual is not an employment contract.

Introduction: Sample Policy
(For Supervisory Personnel)

NOTICE TO SUPERVISORY PERSONNEL

[To be included if a policy manual is distributed to supervisors]

Purpose of policies. This policy manual has been prepared to assist and guide supervisory personnel of (organization) in the administration of (organization's) personnel matters. Adherence to the personnel policies will assure uniformity of personnel practices throughout the organization. Questions about the interpretation of these policies will be addressed to the Executive Director.

Confidentiality and application. This policy manual is for the use of (organization's) supervisory personnel. Its contents will not be made available to anyone else except as authorized by the Executive Director, the Executive Committee, or the Personnel Chair. These policies shall apply to all employees, full-time, part-time, or voluntary.

Authority. Final authority over all personnel policies and practices of (organization) rests with the Board of Directors.

This manual may be amended by the organization at any time. The Personnel Committee is responsible for the preparation and presentation of any new or additional policy development.

All administrative and operational responsibility is vested in the Executive Director, or the volunteer-designee equivalent appointed by the Board of Directors, including responsibility and authority for the administration of approved personnel policies and procedures. Unless specifically limited by the Board of Directors, this includes such actions as employing and dismissing subordinate staff, transferring from one salary grade to another, evaluating worker productivity, and so on. The Executive Director is authorized, at his or her discretion, to delegate some of these authorities, but retains final accountability for any actions taken.

Approval of the Board of Directors is required for creation of new staff positions and changes in pay scales and grade.

No employment contract. These policies are meant to be guidelines only. This manual is not a contract of employment, either express or implied, or a guarantee of future employment for any particular period of time. It is understood that employment with (organization) is deemed to be employment-at-will, whereby either (organization) or the employee has the right to terminate employment for any reason with or without cause and with or without notice or to take any other action regarding employment that is in the best interest of the organization or employee. Any reference in this manual regarding any employment decision which may be taken for a particular purpose is included only to alert employees of (organization's) general policies. They are not intended to limit the discretion of (organization) in making employment decisions.

No employee of (organization) shall be permitted to make oral agreements or assurances contrary to the written provisions of this manual. No person [except _____] has any authority to enter into any agreement for employment for any specified period of time or upon any specific conditions.

NOTICE TO EMPLOYEES [To be included if a policy manual is distributed to employees]

This policy manual has been prepared as a guide and reference for all employees. It is designed to give you an overview and summary of (organization's) policies and procedures currently in effect regarding various employment issues.

(Organization) reserves the right to change these policies and procedures at any time. As policies, procedures, and benefits are revised, these changes will be communicated to you, but advance notice may not always be possible.

No employment contract. The policies and procedures contained in this manual constitute guidelines only. This manual is not a contract of employment, either express or implied, or a guarantee of future employment for any particular period of time. It is understood that employment with the organization is deemed to be employment-at-will, whereby either the organization or the employee has the right to terminate employment for any reason with or without cause and with or without notice or to take any other action regarding employment that is in the organization or employee's best interest. Any reference in this manual regarding any employment decision which may be taken for a particular purpose is included only to alert employees of the organization's general policies. They are not intended to limit the discretion of the organization in making employment decisions.

No employee of the organization shall be permitted to make oral agreements or assurances contrary to the written provisions of this manual. No person [except _____] has any authority to enter into any agreement for employment for any specified period of time or upon any specific conditions.

If you have any questions about this manual or the policies and procedures outlined within it, please contact _____.

2

Equal Employment Opportunity

Discussion

In an equal employment opportunity statement, the organization declares its intention to abide by federal and state discrimination law by making employment decisions (i.e., hiring, promotion, benefits, termination) on a nondiscriminatory basis. Applicants and employees should be judged on their ability to do the job, rather than on impermissible factors such as race, religion, sex and other personal characteristics. Employment procedures should be followed consistently for all employees. For example, verifications of past employment and performance, if conducted, should be conducted for all prospective employees and must be conducted within the parameters of equal employment laws.

Discrimination laws (listed below) directly affect the development of the equal employment policy. Note that state discrimination laws may be broader than the federal law. For example, although the federal law prohibits employment discrimination on the basis of sex, it does not prohibit employment discrimination on the basis of sexual orientation. Moreover, homosexuality or bisexuality are not considered disabilities under federal law. However, some states and municipalities do prohibit discrimination on the basis of sexual orientation. Therefore, state and local law should be checked before drafting an equal employment policy.

Also, not every law listed below applies to every organization. For example, the Americans with Disabilities Act will apply to organizations that have 15 or more employees; it therefore will not apply to smaller organizations. State law may be more restrictive; for example, Connecticut's employment discrimination laws generally apply to employers with three or more employees. In any event, the laws provide a good basis for drafting a policy; however, if you are concerned about the application of specific laws to your organization, you should consult an attorney.

PERTINENT LAWS

• **Civil Rights Act of 1964, Title VII** (prohibits discrimination on the basis of race, color, religion, sex, national origin)

• **Age Discrimination in Employment Act** (prohibits discrimination on the basis of age)

• **Rehabilitation Act of 1973** (prohibits discrimination against the handicapped; applicable to federally funded organizations)

• **Americans with Disabilities Act** (similar to Rehabilitation Act, but applies to virtually all employers)

• **Vietnam Era Veterans Readjustment Act**

• **State discrimination laws**

Equal Employment Opportunity: Sample Policy 1

(Organization) does not discriminate against any individual in regard to any term or condition of employment on account of race, religion, color, gender, national origin, age, disability, veteran [or marital] status, [sexual preference,] or any other reason prohibited by law.

(Organization) supports the principle that each individual should be considered for employment on the basis of his or her ability to perform the tasks of the job in a satisfactory manner and to be treated in a nondiscriminatory manner with respect to performance on the job.

Equal Employment Opportunity: Sample Policy 2
(With Affirmative Action Statement)

(Organization) shall not discriminate against any individual in regard to any term or condition of employment on the basis of race, color, religion, sex, age, disability, national origin, [sexual orientation,] veteran [or marital] status, or any other reason prohibited by law.

(Organization) shall maintain a plan for positive action to achieve equal employment for all persons in the filling of its staff positions. (Organization) shall appoint, annually, an Affirmative Action officer from the senior staff or the Board of Directors

3

Sexual Harassment

Discussion

It is a discriminatory employment practice to harass any job applicant or employee either with words or acts on the basis of sex. *Sexual harassment* is generally defined as unwelcome sexual advances or requests for sexual favors or any conduct of a sexual nature when (1) submission to such conduct is made either implicitly or explicitly a term or condition of the individual's employment; (2) submission to or rejection of such conduct by an individual is used as the basis for employment decisions affecting the individual; or (3) such conduct has the purpose or effect of substantially creating an intimidating, hostile, or offensive working environment. The organization should set up a complaint process whereby certain persons are responsible for investigating complaints. Simply stating that complaints should be referred to the employee's supervisor may not be sufficient, since the supervisor could be the person engaging in harassment.

PERTINENT LAW

- **Civil Rights Act, Title VII**

- **Equal Employment Opportunity Commission regulations**

- **State discrimination and sexual harassment laws**

It has long been the policy of (organization) that all employees have the right to work in an environment free from all types of discrimination, including sexual harassment. (Organization) prohibits sexual harassment of employees in any form. Such conduct may result in disciplinary action up to and including dismissal.

Specifically, no supervisor or member of management shall threaten or insinuate, either explicitly or implicitly, that an employee's refusal to submit to sexual advances will adversely affect the employee's employment, evaluation, wages, advancement, assigned duties, shifts, or any other condition of employment or career development.

Other sexually harassing conduct at the workplace, whether committed by supervisors or by non-supervisory personnel, is also prohibited. This includes repeated offensive language; sexual flirtation; advances; propositions; continual or repeated verbal abuse of a sexual nature; graphic verbal commentaries about an individual's body; sexually suggestive words used to describe an individual; and displays in the workplace of sexually suggestive objects or pictures.

Employees subjected to acts of sexual harassment should immediately inform (specify) or other appropriate persons. Complaints will be examined impartially, and, where merited, appropriate disciplinary action will be taken. Confidentiality will be maintained to the extent permitted by the circumstances.

(Organization) also prohibits retaliation against employees who bring sexual harassment charges or assist in investigating charges. Any employee who brings a sexual harassment complaint or who assists in the investigation of such a complaint will not be adversely affected in terms and conditions of employment, nor be discriminated against or discharged because of the complaint.

4

Job Descriptions

Discussion

Job descriptions inform employees about their duties and form the principle reference for salary development and evaluation. For this reason, job descriptions should be as specific as possible and should identify measurable qualities; they should describe in detail the knowledge, experience, and skill requirements needed to fulfill each job. Job descriptions are derived from the strategic, annual, and program plans. They are developed by the executive or program director as a reflection of the specific goals and tasks which may be established annually to achieve a specific plan.

PERTINENT LAW

• **Americans with Disabilities Act (ADA):** The ADA prohibits discrimination against otherwise qualified individuals who have a disability. An individual is otherwise qualified if he or she can perform the essential functions of a job, with or without reasonable accommodation. Although the ADA does not require employers to establish written job descriptions, such descriptions will be considered as evidence of essential functions and will help the employer and the disabled individual determine whether the individual is in fact otherwise qualified for the position that he or she holds or seeks.

Job Descriptions: Sample Policy

(Organization) maintains written job descriptions for each position within the organization. Each job description consists of a brief definition of the position and examples of specific duties. The level of education, experience, knowledge, skills, and abilities considered important for successful performance are also included within each job description.

The Executive Director of (organization) is responsible for developing job descriptions for all existing and new positions. He or she shall review these descriptions annually and modify them as necessary to ensure their accuracy. The Board, through the Personnel Committee, will periodically review and modify the Executive Director's job description. Such job descriptions are intended for administrative use and are not part of these personnel policies.

5

Hiring of New Employees

Discussion

Occasionally, owing to expansion of the organization, retirement of an employee, transfer and promotion, and so on, specific jobs become open. The organization should have a policy and procedure which describes how vacancies shall be filled.

Hiring of New Employees: Sample Policy

When there are job openings within (organization), it is the organization's desire and intention to fill the open position with the best possible candidate, giving special consideration to any present employees who express an interest in and are qualified for the position. Job openings and promotions will therefore generally be posted so that all interested employees may apply.

Hiring of New Employees: Sample Procedure
(Guidelines for Managers)

Process

The vacancy shall be defined and classified within the guidelines and policies of the organization and affirmative action requirements. Requirements and qualifications shall also be made known. All means should be used to communicate a position's availability, including internal postings, paid advertising, direct mail, community bulletin boards, word-of-mouth, and other appropriate resources (optionally including personnel specialists).

Time-line

Unless the vacancy must be filled immediately, the vacancy shall be publicized for at least two weeks.

Closing Date

There shall be a specific closing date for the vacancy, and all candidates shall be notified that their applications have been received.

Review Process

There shall be a review process which is uniform for all candidates.

Interview

Several of the most qualified candidates shall be interviewed and their credentials and references verified. If deemed appropriate, (organization) may seek references beyond those provided by the candidate. [NOTE: It is illegal to require information concerning nationality, family, race, religion, sex, sexual preference, disability, or arrest record. Language ability, credit and conviction records, and discrimination-related issues may be pursued only if related directly to the job or otherwise required by law.]

Hiring & Notification

Upon agreement with a finalist, notification shall be made to all candidates of the outcome. On or prior to the starting date, information concerning salary and benefits, job description, full-time equivalent (FTE), probationary period and evaluation, orientation and on-the-job (or specialized) training, and the personnel manual will be provided. All applications must remain on file for at least six months, and may be re-screened if a new hire fails to workout during this time.

6

Job Classification, Scheduling, and Salaries

Discussion

This section is used to classify employment status for the purpose of consistently determining payment levels and benefits. Among the possible classifications are part-time, full-time, temporary, salaried, non-salaried, exempt, non-exempt and volunteer. Note that the fact that an individual receives a salary does not necessarily mean that the individual may be classified as an exempt employee under state and federal wage and hour laws. This section also covers scheduling procedures and salary issues.

PERTINENT LAWS

- **Fair Labor Standards Act of 1938/1977**

- **Equal Pay Act of 1963**

Job Classification, Scheduling, and Salaries:
Sample Policy (Salaried vs. Non-Salaried)

For the purposes of determining benefits employees will be classified as either salaried or non-salaried.

Salaried employees are classified into two sub-classifications: full-time or part-time. Full-time salaried employees are those personnel who work 35 hours or more weekly. Part-time salaried personnel are those who work fewer than 35 hours and more than 20 hours per week.

Non-salaried personnel are those personnel who are hired on an hourly basis. They do not receive benefits.

Job Classification, Scheduling, and Salaries: Sample Policy (Exempt vs. Non-Exempt)

(Organization) designates two categories of staff: exempt and non-exempt.

Exempt employees. Executive, professional, and administrative personnel are exempt from the minimum wage and overtime requirements of the Fair Labor Standards Act.

Exempt employees are considered upper management, as specified by state and federal employment fair practices. There is no provision for overtime pay for exempt employees, and no requests for reimbursement shall be honored. However, management may schedule flexible hours.

Non-exempt employees. All other employees are non-exempt. Non-exempt employees are considered regular staff and are subject to the minimum wage and overtime requirements as specified by state and federal wage and hour laws.

Volunteers are staff whose employment and/or position is unpaid and is generally of a temporary nature (lasting less than 6 months). Volunteers are not eligible for any benefits or compensation other than approved and job-related expenses. However, they will be protected by all other non-salary and non-benefit guidelines of these Personnel Policies.

The following describes work-week and scheduling procedures:

Work-week Length

(Organization) has a 35- or 40-hour regular work week. Office hours may vary according to the prevailing practice in the area served by the office. Employees shall be informed by the supervisor of any variance existing at the time of employment or occurring at any time thereafter.

Lunch Scheduling

All employees who work 35- or 40-hours a week will be given a one-hour lunch break daily. The supervisor is responsible for scheduling lunch. Every effort will be made to accommodate employee preferences while maintaining agency availability to those seeking service.

Breaks

All employees who work 35- or 40-hours a week will be given two, 15-minute breaks per day.

Overtime

Overtime pay, at one and a half times the rate of regular pay, will be paid to all non-exempt employees for hours worked beyond the regular 40-hour work week.

Flextime

Where practical for (organization) and approved by the immediate supervisor, exempt employees will be allowed a flexible scheduling of work hours.

A salary and wage schedule provides for rates of pay related to the function and level of responsibility for each job description. The salary grade and organizational table of salary increments will be reviewed annually by the Personnel Committee and their recommendations submitted to the Board of Directors for its approval.

Beginning Salaries

New staff members are appointed at minimum starting salary. In special circumstances (e.g., to secure the services of persons with exceptional abilities and experience) appointments may be made at appropriate pay above this starting salary.

In-Range Salary Increases

Salary increase is not automatic; a raise in pay is based on excellence of worker performance and evidence of growing productivity. Cost of living indices may also be used in considering wage and salary increases.

Once a year the Budget and Finance and Personnel Committees will review the entire salary structure and will review and make a recommendation to the Board of Directors on the Executive Director's salary.

Salary Changes Accompanying Changes in Status

When an employee transfers to a position paid in the same salary grade as the former position, pay rate will remain the same. The employee may be granted a one-step increase within the range, at the Executive Director's discretion.

When a worker is placed in a lower salary range for any reason (e.g., position reclassification, position changes due to reduction in force, demotion, etc.), a salary decrease to the equivalent step in the lower range may occur. In all such instances, new dates for salary review may be established.

Pay Periods

Salaries and wages are paid the 15th and the last day of each month. [NOTE: This practice may be illegal under state law; in Connecticut, for example, wages must be paid weekly unless an alternative schedule is approved by the Commissioner of Labor.]

Pay Advances

Payments of salaries may be made in advance for leaves or emergency purposes. Requests for pay advances must be made in writing to the Supervisor. Requests for leave advances must be made by the day before the pay period closest to the leave.

Payroll Deductions

Federal and state income tax is withheld from wages, as required by law. A statement of earnings and deductions, to use to file income tax returns, will be sent to each employee prior to January 31 of each year. Federal Social Security tax and other deductions, as may be set by law, are also deducted and reported accordingly.

7

Performance Appraisal

Discussion

Each employee needs to know where he or she stands with the organization and what is expected of him or her. The section on evaluation describes the organization's commitment to measure the effectiveness of employees and to consider this measurement in light of employment status. Frequency of evaluation should be specified. Persons responsible for reviews may be identified.

Performance Appraisal: Sample Policy
(Focuses on Review)

The performance of an employee will be reviewed at the end of three months, twelve months, and at least annually thereafter so that an employee shall have a minimum of one formal performance review each year. Such review shall include a written evaluation of the employee's performance. The Executive Director's review shall take place at the stated intervals and shall also include a written evaluation.

Performance Appraisal: Sample Policy
(More Detailed; Includes Orientation and Training as well as Review Procedures)

Introduction. At the beginning of employment each new staff member will be given both a copy of these policies and information stating the origin and purpose of (organization); the relationship of (organization) to other community agencies/groups; the duties and responsibilities of the new employee; the relation of those duties to other employees and volunteers; and instructions necessary for sound initial performance.

Staff will be given reasonable opportunity to participate in staff meetings and other agency meetings and to attend training workshops and conferences, as appropriate.

Probationary Period. For exempt and non-exempt personnel the probationary period is three months. During this time, employees have the opportunity to become accustomed to their work and to enhance their performance on the job. Before the end of the probationary period, the employee's performance will be reviewed with him/her by the immediate supervisor. A probationary period may be extended for up to 45 days.

Performance Appraisal. An evaluation of each employee's performance will be made at least once a year after the probationary period. The evaluation may be used as a basis for task changes, a realignment of duties, promotion, termination, or salary and wage adjustment.

Factors to be considered include dependability, initiative, responsibility, and ability to understand and interpret (organization's) policies.

The immediate supervisor will discuss the evaluation appraisal with the employee, providing an opportunity to address areas of concern. The employee may submit his or her written statement of agreement or disagreement with the evaluation, and will be given a copy of the evaluation. A copy is retained in the personnel file.

An annual review of the performance of the Executive Director will be made by the Personnel Committee and shall include an appraisal of his or her adherence to (organization's) an annual performance plan.

Promotions. Preference will be given to promoting current employees of (organization). Promotions will be based on an employee's ability to perform the duties listed in the job description.

8

Disciplinary Action

Discussion

In this section, a board describes its commitment to conflict resolution. The board can make clear which responses it will consider when an employee reports that a disciplinary action was unfair or applied in a discriminatory manner. This policy may specify the nature of the problems which are open for resolution. This policy also specifies the limits of the board and executive director.

This policy must be consistent with affirmative action statements. The board may also wish to adopt corresponding disciplinary or grievance procedures which outline the specific steps to be followed, such as when, how, and to whom objections should be submitted and any appeal processes.

Disciplinary Action: Sample Policy

All employees are expected to meet (organization's) standards for work performance, punctuality, attendance, and personal conduct. When an employee fails to conform to expected standards, the organization shall endeavor to give the employee notice and an opportunity to correct the deficiency. If performance does not improve, the disciplinary steps set forth below may be instituted.

(Organization) hopes that all employees will respect one another and cooperate on work projects. (Organization) recognizes, however, that personality clashes and other conflicts may occur. All efforts should be made to resolve personnel conflicts through supervisors or the Executive Director. When an issue is not resolvable within the staffing structure, appeal in accordance with the grievance procedure should be instituted. The Board of Directors of (organization) has the final responsibility for addressing all occasions of personnel-related conflict by its employees.

The following describes the steps and procedures for disciplinary action.

Verbal Warning

In the event of misconduct, a verbal warning may be given, along with a personnel memo citing time and date, situation, means, and timeliness of correction. Verbal warnings cannot be included as a part of an employee's personnel file.

Reprimand

In the event of a second occurrence, a written reprimand may be given in a meeting with the employee in question, citing time and date, situation, means, and timeliness of correction. This reprimand shall become a part of the personnel file of the individual cited.

With a reprimand on file, any further violation shall be construed as grounds for another reprimand, in writing.

Two or more written reprimands may be grounds for probation, suspension, or dismissal.

Reprimands shall be removed from the personnel file after two years from the occurrence.

Grievance

A grievance is a request by an employee or group of employees for relief in a matter concerning dissatisfaction with the work situation, discrimination, or harassment.

Grievance Procedure

Grievances must be submitted in writing to the Executive Director within thirty days of the date the person filing the grievance becomes aware of the alleged action which causes the grievance.

A grievance must be in writing, signed by the grieving

party and contain the problem or action and the remedy or relief sought.

The Executive Director shall investigate the grievance within seven days after the date the grievance is filed. The investigation may be informal; however, it shall be thorough.

The Executive Director will issue a written decision on the grievance within twelve days of the filing. This written decision will be filed with the chair of the Personnel Committee and a copy given to the complainant.

Appeal

Persons filing a grievance may appeal the decision of the Executive Director within fifteen days after a written decision is rendered. The appeal shall be addressed to the Personnel Committee.

The Personnel Committee of the Board of Directors shall convene a subcommittee of the Personnel Committee to hear the appeal. All interested parties may be invited to be present. The ruling of this committee shall be given within fourteen days of the hearing and shall be final for the organization.

9

Benefits Administration

Discussion

A benefit is broadly defined as "anything contributing to an improvement in condition." Benefits provide employees with an added ability and incentive to perform their jobs beyond what a wage or salary accomplishes. If a benefits program is successful, employees will have an increased ability to meet their needs and will, in turn, be more productive.

Some benefits are required by law (e.g., Social Security). Benefits may be direct or indirect. Health insurance is a direct benefit (which an employee can gain immediately). Worker's compensation and unemployment compensation are indirect benefits but obviously, if needed, may produce direct benefits.

Rather than identifying specific benefits, which are subject to change and are best described in separate benefits documents, the personnel policies generally state the types of benefits which the organization will provide as a part of employment.

Beyond the traditional benefits (i.e., health and life insurance), employee assistance programs, insurance menus, day care, and pensions may be considered.

PERTINENT LAW

- **Social Security Act**
- **Unemployment Compensation**

- **Worker's Compensation laws**

- **Employee Retirement Income Security Act (ERISA)**, as amended by the **Consolidated Omnibus Budget Reconciliation Act (COBRA)**

- **Discrimination laws** (see also Equal Employment Opportunity section, above; these laws generally prohibit discrimination in all terms and conditions of employment, which includes benefits)

(Organization) is committed to providing all employees with the benefits afforded them by law. Depending on available resources, (organization) may provide all employees with additional benefits, such as health and life insurance, which will enhance and encourage long-term commitment to the organization.

Notwithstanding anything in this manual, the specific provisions of any insurance policy govern. (Organization) will furnish to individual participants in the insurance programs any required summary plan descriptions or other documents as may be required by law. If you have any questions regarding the benefits offered by the organization, please contact (specify title).

(Organization) urges you to take advantage of all insurances which are offered, and for which you are eligible, especially if you do not have similar coverage elsewhere. However, it is your decision to waive coverage if you so desire. If you choose to waive any of the insurance coverages offered, you will be asked to sign a waiver of insurance card to protect both you and the organization. In some cases (Organization) may offer an additional option.

10

Attendance, Vacations, and Leaves of Absence

Discussion

Policies on attendance and leaves must be stated to alleviate doubt as to when an employee will or will not be paid for an absence. Organizational budget and values are reflected in policies. For example, paternity leave policies reflect an organization's values regarding the role of the father in child development and family responsibility. Note that while some employee leaves of absence are required by law (e.g., jury duty), others (e.g., for professional development, personal days) are at the discretion of the employer.

PERTINENT LAW

The federal government has considered but has not yet adopted a family leave law. However, some states do have a family leave law, which outlines the conditions under which an employee may take leave for family reasons and the employee's status and right to benefits and compensation when on such leave. Also, various state and federal laws may govern whether employees are paid for holidays, sick time, jury duty, and disability leaves, as well as the rights of employees to return to work after an absence.

(Organization) expects all employees to give a productive day's work, to arrive at (organization) and begin work on time, and to leave work no earlier than the scheduled closing or quitting time. However, (organization) recognizes that a normal amount of employee sickness or disability will occur during each year, and that employees may need to take time off from work because of sickness or disability. Also, (organization) recognizes that employees should receive time off for vacation and other personal reasons, as well as any leaves which may be required by law. For these reasons, the organization has adopted the following policy and procedures regarding employee leaves of absence:

Unpaid Leaves of Absence

Administrative leave. Unpaid leaves of absence may be granted by (organization) in instances where unusual or unavoidable circumstances require an employee's absence. Such unpaid leaves are granted on the assumption that an employee will be available to return to regular employment when the conditions necessitating the leave permit.

If the Executive Director determines that the requirements of (organization) necessitate that the position be filled, the Executive Director shall notify the employee that circumstances require the employee to return to the position, accept alternate employment or layoff upon return, or terminate his or her employment. During any unpaid leave, the employee shall not receive any benefits, except that individuals on parental leave may receive health insurance coverage or additional coverage as specified in these policies.

Leaves of absence will not be computed as part of the employee's length of service with (organization). Failure to return to work at the end of a leave of absence or provide approved documentation for extension prior to that time will be considered resignation by the employee.

Family leave. To assist in the nurturing and development of a new infant or child in an employee's family, (organization) will provide two months of unpaid leave with guaranteed reinstatement into the employee's former position unless there is a substantial change in fiscal operating circumstances that would have resulted in the elimination of such position in the regular course of operations. For a woman who took pregnancy disability leave, this leave begins following her disability leave; otherwise, it begins when the employee leaves his or her work activities and shall run consecutively. During such period of unpaid leave, (organization) shall continue to provide the same health care coverage the employee would normally have received from (organization).

Employees may apply accumulated vacation time toward parental leave. When such paid time is applied the employee will continue to accrue regular vacation for this period only.

The employee shall, where practical, provide at least four weeks' notice of his or her intent to return.

Paid Leaves of Absences

Employees may be entitled to a paid leave of absence, in accordance with the following conditions:

Sick leave. Sick days are to be used only for personal illness or injury "off the job." Employees who are repeatedly absent or absent for five or more consecutive days in any calendar year because of illness may be required to submit a written statement from the attending physician verifying illness to the Executive Director.

Up to ten working days with pay in a twelve-month period will be available to full-time employees for illness. Sick leave is accrued on a monthly basis. Sick leave may not be used before it is accrued, and it may not be used until an employee has completed 90 days of full-time continuous employment. Sick leave may be accrued up to but may not exceed 20 days. Sick days are not "earned," and employees will not be paid for unused sick days upon termination of employment.

Any employee using sick days must telephone his or her immediate supervisor during the first fifteen minutes of the scheduled work day, if possible. The supervisor or person designated to act in the supervisor's absence must receive the call from the employee. If an employee does not call in on the day of absence, the employee will not be paid. In cases of extreme emergency, the call may be made by a family member. Failure to report could lead to termination.

Reasonable Accomodation. Every attempt will be made by (organization) to protect the tenure of valued employees during health crisis. In the event of a partial or temporary disability, an employee may reduce to part-time employment or job-sharing with another employee, if the organization's requirements permit this. [NOTE: Under the Americans with Disabilities Act, a reduction of hours or change of responsibilities may be required as a reasonable accommodation.] Employees may also request unpaid administrative leave, or join other employees who agree to pool and share accumulated sick leave.

Personal days. With supervisory approval, full-time employees are allowed three absences in a twelve-month period, with pay, for observance of religious holidays or for other personal reasons, including family illness, inability to get to work due to car trouble or weather when (organization) is open for business, and household matters. The following general rules apply to the use of personal days:
• One must have been employed a minimum of 90 days to be eligible (eligibility requirements will be waived for

employees observing religious holidays).
• Personal days are earned at the rate of one day for every four months of full-time employment.
• Personal days may not be used before they are earned.
• Personal days may be taken in half-day units.
• Personal days may be taken consecutively, with approval by the department head or supervisor.

Jury duty. Jury duty is regarded as a citizenship obligation. An employee called for jury duty is extended a leave of absence for the duration of jury service. Employees are required to report for work on business days when released from jury duty temporarily or when sessions are postponed. Only the difference between regular salary and judicial compensation will be paid, unless the law requires otherwise.

Professional development. Employees are encouraged to participate in special conferences, workshops, seminars, and the like designed for continuous upgrading of skills and competencies. The Executive Director will use his or her discretion in granting time for attendance at such activities.

Military leave. Any employee inducted into active military service will be granted a leave of absence without pay. Re-employment will be provided upon return to civilian life, provided application for re-employment is completed within 90 days of leaving active service, or as otherwise required by law.

Any employee required to participate in annual military training programs as a member of the Armed Forces Reserves will be granted up to two weeks of military leave annually. During this period of absence, the organization will pay the difference between the employee's regular salary and the military base pay (if the latter is smaller). If the military pay exceeds the (organization) salary, then the military leave will be considered a leave without pay.

Compensatory time for exempt employees. When an exempt employee is requested or required to work longer than 45 hours within a given week, that employee may take a paid leave of equal time within (specify) days following the extended work week. Notification of extended hours and of planned absence must be given in writing to the employee's immediate supervisor, and the supervisor must approve the time off. Compensatory time may not be approved within two successive pay periods.

Paid holidays. A total of ten holidays will be offered. Nine are designated; one is floating or at the discretion of the employer. All employees are entitled to take the following paid holidays, except that if a holiday falls on a weekday on which a part-time employee does not work, that employee will not be paid for that holiday. Full payment for holiday time will be provided to full-time staff. Salaried part-time employees are eligible for pro-rated reimbursement based on an average number of hours worked in a twelve-month period.

> January - New Year's Day
> February - Presidents' Day
> May - Memorial Day
> July - Independence Day
> September - Labor Day
> November - Thanksgiving Day, Friday after
>   Thanksgiving Day
> December - Religious Observance
> Tenth holiday (organization's choice)

A legal holiday which falls on Saturday will be observed on the preceding Friday. Legal holidays which fall on Sunday will be observed on the following Monday.

If a holiday falls on a day during a staff member's vacation, an extra day is allowed and generally may be taken with the vacation; with the Executive Director's permission, it may be taken later in the year. If religious holidays which staff members wish to observe fall on days other than the above, time shall be made up out of vacation time or on some other planned basis.

Vacation. After the employee has completed six months of full-time continuous service, the employee is entitled to five paid vacation days.

Upon completion of one year of full-time continuous service, the employee is entitled to five additional paid vacation days.

The beginning of the employee's second year of full-time continuous service the employee is entitled to twelve paid vacation days annually.

The beginning of the employee's third year of full-time continuous service, the employee is entitled to fifteen paid vacation days annually.

The beginning of the employee's fifth year of full-time continuous service, the employee is entitled to twenty paid vacation days annually.

Vacation time may not be accrued for more than one year. Vacation time must be approved in advance by the employee's supervisor.

Holidays observed by the organization and occurring during an employee's vacation period will not be counted against vacation time.

Advance payment of salary must be requested in writing if a payday falls on a vacation day.

No vacation time is earned during the portion of a leave of absence, sick leave, or disability extending beyond one month.

No pay is given in lieu of vacation except upon retirement or termination of employment.

Bereavement. Employees will be allowed up to three days off, with pay, in the event of the death of members of their immediate family. Immediate family is defined as consisting of spouse or domestic partner, mother, father, mother-in-law, father-in-law, children, brothers, sisters, and grandparents.

Any additional time off needed may be taken without pay from (organization) upon a supervisor's approval, or with pay against unused personal or vacation days.

11

Expense Reimbursement

Discussion

An organization must be clear about when it will reimburse an employee for expenses to alleviate potential confusion and inconsistency. Reimbursement policies reflect an organization's financial capacity and contract provisions but also reflect values regarding the activities or efforts of employees. For example, reimbursement of full educational expenses reflects the organization's commitment to support academic pursuits.

General

All normal and legitimate business expenses are paid directly by (organization) or are reimbursed, provided prior authorization has been given for such expenditures. Reimbursement for all authorized business expenses must be supported by itemized signed vouchers on forms approved by the Executive Director. Also, requests for reimbursement for all expenses must be accompanied by a receipt or other appropriate documentation.

Travel and Telephone Expenses

Reimbursement for mileage will be paid at the federal (or state where applicable) rate per mile. Tolls and parking fees are reimbursable.

Reimbursable mileage is computed from office location. Only that mileage over daily drive to and from work is reimbursable.

Reasonable cost for long-distance telephone calls are reimbursable. If calls are made from a home phone, the request for reimbursement must be accompanied by a copy of the telephone bill.

Meals

Reasonable costs for meals are reimbursable. Such costs might be incurred because the employee is unavoidably away from the office or home at mealtime or is attending a lunch or dinner that is work related.

Conference and Other Expenses

Reasonable expenses for food, lodging, and registration are reimbursable. Supplies, refreshments, and postage are also reimbursable.

The following describes the specific allowable expenses for which reimbursement may be requested by an employee and the process for obtaining reimbursement.

Authorized Expenses

On trips within the employee's geographic area of responsibility the following necessary expenses incurred for business purposes are authorized for reimbursement:

1. Employee's auto mileage in excess of normal daily commuting mileage (distance between employee's home and organization's office); reimbursement is currently (specify) cents per mile. Volunteer employees should keep records of auto mileage incurred on organization business for the allowable deduction on income tax returns. Volunteer and paid employees will pay all operational and maintenance expenses of their personal cars during organization business, including maintaining all required insurance coverage. (NOTE: The Internal Revenue Service establishes allowable deductible rates.)

2. Parking fees

3. Bridge and toll fees in excess of those required in normal commuting

4. Taxi or mass transit fares

5. Postage and telephone expenses for organization business

6. Entertainment expenses as pre-approved by the employee's supervisor.

Extended Travel

On trips where an employee or volunteer remains away from home overnight, the same expenses listed in Section 1 are authorized for reimbursement. In addition, the following shall apply:

1. Cost of air or train fare incurred at the lowest available rate. Super-saver fares or similar cost-saving plans should be used when time permits; in no case will the reimbursement exceed the cost of coach airfare.

2. Car rental, only if no other less expensive transportation is available. Car rental agency insurance is not reimbursable.

3. Hotel or motel costs not to exceed published commercial rates for a single room. When the employee is attending a meeting or conference for which a group hotel rate has been obtained, the reimbursement will not exceed the group rate.

4. Employees will be reimbursed for meals at actual cost, with proper documentation but not to exceed $40 per day. A $40 per diem meal allowance for extended travel may be allowed with prior approval by the Executive Director. (When one or more meals is provided in connection with a meeting or conference, the daily meal allowance will be reduced by the appropriate amount.)

Entertainment

Entertainment expenses may be reimbursed with the prior approval of the Executive Director or his or her designee, but shall be confined to employees and volunteers whose job function clearly warrants entertainment. Entertainment should be kept to a reasonable level in conformity to the business relationship and related to a business meeting or discussion from which (organization) will benefit directly. Each entertainment expense for (organization) is to be shown separately on the expense voucher and must be properly documented.

Volunteers

Volunteers may submit properly documented expenses for items as described under the category "Authorized Expenses" and for the cost of meals not to exceed $____ per day. The Executive Director or Board designee must give prior approval for these expenses.

Non-Reimbursable Expenses

Some normally non-reimbursable expenses may be reimbursed upon full written explanation and request to the Executive Director (or Board President in the place of the Executive Director). Such items which may be considered for reimbursement include out-of-town laundry service, room services, some extra-ordinary transportation. Note, however, that these items will be reimbursed only in the most unusual cases, and the Executive Director has complete discretion to determine whether such expenses will be reimbursed.

Expense Vouchers and Reporting

Expense Vouchers:

1. All expenses must be pre-approved.

2. Employees will submit documentation for all expense reimbursement requests using the "Weekly Report Form."

3. Volunteers, officers and directors will submit all documentation for all expense reimbursement requests using the "Officer/Director/Volunteer Expense Voucher."

When part of an expenditure is personal in nature, the explanation should be written on the form for which reimbursement is being requested.

Timeliness

Timely processing of expense vouchers is important to assure that expenses are included in the accounting period for which they were incurred.

Employees or volunteers incurring expenses on behalf of (organization) shall submit an expense voucher with receipts at least once a month and one pay period from the time expenses are incurred.

Reimbursement will be made by check, as soon as vouchers have been reviewed and approved for the next pay period.

12

Termination of Employment

Discussion

As employees and employers make choices to begin an employment relationship, so do employees and employers make choices to end an employment relationship. The rules for ending an employment relationship must be as clear as those for beginning the relationship. This is particularly true when the occasion for ending a relationship is not positive for either or both parties.

PERTINENT LAW

• Possible employee claims for wrongful discharge (including employer retaliation because employee exercised protected rights), discrimination, defamation, breach of contract **Federal Civil Rights Acts/Title VII;** other discrimination laws.

All employment with (organization) is "at will," which means that any employee may terminate his or her employment for any reason at any time; likewise, the employer may terminate any employee's employment at any time without notice. The Executive Director may, but is not required to, warn an employee of any problem in order to give the employee the ability to correct the problem, and the Executive Director may, but is not required to, place an employee on probation under such terms and conditions as the Executive Director may determine are appropriate under the circumstances.

Procedures for Leaving (Organization) Service

Resignations. Exempt staff are requested to submit a letter of resignation to the Executive Director thirty (30) days in advance of planned departure. Non-exempt staff are requested to submit a letter of resignation to the Executive Director two weeks prior to planned departure.

Termination. The organization shall endeavor to give reasonable notice to an employee prior to termination; however, the organization reserves the right to terminate employees immediately for insubordination, dishonesty, harassment, embezzlement, intoxication, or for causing dissension among other employees or volunteers.

Layoff. Employees may be laid off with notice determined by the Executive Director. All accrued benefits shall be honored. Layoffs may be temporary.

Departure for health reasons. Staff who separate from (organization) because of health reasons, voluntarily or involuntarily, shall do so following an exit interview involving the Executive Director or Personnel Committee Chair, and shall do so consistent with the availability of benefits due them relevant to their position as staff.

Exit Interviews and Related Information

An exit interview will be conducted with all departing employees, whether the employee is terminated by (organization) or leaves voluntarily. The Executive Director or immediate supervisor will conduct such interviews. The President of the Board or Chair of the Personnel Committee of the Board will conduct the exit interview of the Executive Director.

An employee who resigns or is terminated shall be informed of available health benefits under COBRA or related laws prior to or during the exit interview.

An employee who resigns or is terminated and who has not used earned vacation will receive vacation pay as accrued up to the date of termination. An employer may elect to use accrued vacation in lieu of the pre-termination period.

Every employee leaving the service of (organization) will surrender keys, working equipment, and money or other property belonging to (organization). Failure to do so may result in financial penalties resulting from re-keying locks and re-securing other restricted access areas.

13

Privacy Code

Discussion

An organization needs to know certain personal information about its employees. For example, an organization may need certain information in order to provide insurance. In addition, an organization also may be required by state or federal law to elicit certain information from its employees. For example, the Internal Revenue Service may require certain identifying information for payroll and tax purposes. The organization, therefore, must balance its "need to know" with the employee's right to privacy.

PERTINENT LAW

- **Freedom of Information Act**

- **State laws dealing with personnel files**

Other laws restricting employer's access to certain information (i.e., the **Americans with Disabilities Act**; discrimination laws which prohibit certain inquiries)

Possible employee claims of defamation, invasion of privacy

(Organization) may collect, retain, and use any information about each employee which is deemed necessary, except as prohibited by law. (Organization) respects each employee's right to privacy and will protect and preserve the confidentiality of all personal information in its records or files.

Personnel Records

A personnel record is maintained by (organization) for each employee. This record shall contain:

- Employee's completed employment application
- Employee's current and previous job descriptions (including notice of outside work)
- Employee's performance summaries
- Employee's salary history
- Employee's medical record for insurance purposes [NOTE: This should be kept in a separate file, apart from other personal information.]
- Employee's record of current accrued vacation, sick and compensatory time
- Current resume, vita

The personnel record is open and available to the employee for inspection by appointment. A copy of any part of or the whole record will be provided to the employee at the employee's own expense, but the employee may not remove anything from his or her personnel file except as specifically authorized by the (specify title). Each employee has the right to correct or request deletion of inaccurate information, and may request permission to include a note of disagreement if there is conflict.

Each personnel file is confidential. Personnel files shall be kept in a locked, secure location. Information from the file is available only to the (specify title), (organization) employees with a business need to know (as determined by the Executive Director), and those authorized by the employee.

Disclosure of Information to Others

Disclosure of information about an employee may not be made to people or organizations outside (organization) without the employee's written authorization, except as may be required or permitted by law.

To protect the privacy of all concerned, all (organization) personnel should direct incoming inquiries regarding credit reference or employment verification for present or former paid employees to the Executive Director. Verification of former employment with (organization) shall be limited to title, salary, and duration of tenure with (organization). Any other information shall be given only if legally required or approved in writing by the employee in question.

14

Workplace Health and Safety

Discussion

An organization should strive to protect the health and safety of its employees and also should comply with state and federal laws regulating workplace safety.

PERTINENT LAW

- **Occupational Health & Safety (OSHA) laws and regulations**

- **State health and safety laws, smoking laws**

(Organization) is committed to providing a safe, healthy, and comfortable workplace for all its employees, clients, and guests. A clean work area makes for a more pleasant, as well as a safer, place to work. Employees are asked to help keep the surroundings as neat and orderly as possible.

Employees will be provided with instructions regarding procedures to be followed in the event of fire or other emergencies. Employees are encouraged to be conscious of health and safety, and are expected to comply with all safety and health requirements, whether established by (organization) or by federal, state, or local law. Employees should report any unsafe conditions or circumstances to their supervisor or safety coordinator.

Illnesses and Injuries

Job-related injuries and illnesses, regardless of severity, should be reported as soon as possible to a supervisor or safety coordinator so that the injury or illness can be evaluated and medical attention provided if necessary.

Smoking

(Organization) wishes to provide a smoke-free environment for its employees. No smoking is permitted in the building except where otherwise designated [or specific site(s) may be named]. *Smoking* includes the burning of a lighted cigar, cigarette, pipe, or any other matter or substance which contains tobacco. The organization shall not discriminate against those employees who do smoke outside of work. [NOTE: Smoking is usually covered by state law, so you should check the law before establishing a smoking policy.]

Horseplay

Horseplay and practical joking can result in serious injuries or death; therefore, anyone engaging in horseplay or practical joking will be subject to discipline up to and including termination.

The Emergency Preparedness Plan is designed to prevent injury and loss to employees, clients, volunteers, visitors, facilities, and property during and after a crisis; to improve the emergency management process; and to permit an expedient return to normal operations.

The Emergency Preparedness Plan is to be in effect 24 hours a day, 7 days a week in order to react effectively to any emergency conditions which might affect the agency, its employees, clients, volunteers, visitors, facilities, or property.

Threat Analysis

In the selection of office or program service sites, every effort must be expended to understand the sites structural integrity as well as the area's history and level of risk in regard to earthquakes, floods, tornadoes, hurricanes, fires, and other natural disasters.

Proper emergency equipment, evacuation procedures, and compliance with local codes must be prepared and available for reference and use in case of a threat. Evacuation and emergency procedures must highlight the location and availability of security systems, emergency exits, emergency power systems, warning systems, and safety systems.

Building Population

Receptionists and other key representatives must be aware of building occupants at all times—especially individuals with physical challenges. Switchboard functions as well as individuals skilled in first aid, and special needs must be identified, in advance, and available for service in the event of an emergency.

Knowledge of other tenants in the facility must be known and posted at reception and emergency exits and included in emergency triage procedures.

Triage

1. Information. The location of, and access to, hospitals, shelters, police, fire, and emergency services must be posted and known by key persons.

2. Evacuation. Major and secondary evacuation routes must be identified in advance.

3. Networking. An off-site contact person and place must be secured in the event of a disaster. A telephone list for identifying the location of missing persons must be available as well as posted, on site. If needed, an RV is helpful. Often an out-of-area telephone contact or voice-mail is an emergency contact asset

Chain of Command

For the purpose of emergency preparedness and reaction, an organizational plan may require a chain of command. Suggested methodology for this is as follows:
1. Executive/Associate Director, Board Chairperson/Vice President
2. Administrative Assistant, Office Manager, or Receptionist
3. Senior Program Staff, Patient, or Volunteer Coordinator

Staff and board members must be accountable for check-in following an emergency, to ascertain their well-being and whereabouts, as well as to enlist assistance, when required. This includes knowledge and use of out-of-area contact when needed. A checklist of employees is to be kept up-to-date.

Patient Care

Patient care, when involved, assumes priority over all other obligations, personal and professional. Referral is of utmost importance following an immobilizing event. This must include, by prearranged agreement with clients, necessary records, needs and requirements, and referral log and follow-up.

Family and loved ones should also be a part of the follow-up notification system in the event of an emergency, therefore current contact information should be on record, in advance.

Emergency Action Check List

Leadership must also secure emergency shut-down procedures, damage control and assessment, especially as it relates to individuals, and security precautions. For the purpose of emergency leadership, a checklist of available resources and responsibilities must be developed. Potentials for inclusion are the following:

1. Evacuation procedure and accomplishment
2. Electric, gas, and water shutoff
3. Retrieval of priority items and client records
4. Identifying location and well being of all affected individuals

First Aid

A first aid kit approved by the Red Cross must be accessible from all exits and emergency evacuation locations. This must be supplemented by radio, preferably CB, with batteries, blankets, rechargeable flashlights, fresh bottled water, plastic gloves, work gloves, soap, tissue, tape, pen, paper, trash bags, knife, and matches.

15

Substance Abuse

Discussion

Alcohol and drug abuse (including prescription drug abuse) is an increasing problem at the workplace. This policy focuses on the individual's right to work in a healthy environment and an organization's need to ensure alert, responsible employees, prevent accidents, and protect co-workers and clients from intoxicated employees.

PERTINENT LAWS

• **Federal Drug-Free Workplace Act**

• **Occupational Safety and Health laws and regulations**

• **Americans with Disabilities Act** (NOTE: Alcoholism is a disability under the ADA, although alcoholics may be held to the same attendance and performance standards as other employees. The ADA also protects recovering substance abusers, although current users of illegal drugs are not protected.)

• **State laws regarding substance abuse, drug testing**

The distribution, possession, and/or use of controlled substances will not be tolerated in or around the worksite at any time, or while an employee is acting in furtherance of (organization) business.

Employees who have controlled substances legally prescribed to them by a licensed health-care professional shall use such controlled substances only in the manner, combination, and quantity prescribed. If using the prescribed substance affects job performance, the employee should report this to his or her supervisor and may be required to take medical leave. The use of a controlled substance as part of a prescribed medical treatment is not grounds for disciplinary action, but it is important for (organization) to know that the use is occurring. It may be necessary to change an employee's job assignment while the employee is undergoing treatment. All information provided by the employee or health-care professional regarding prescribed medical treatment will be kept in strictest confidence.

Possessing or consuming alcoholic beverages at the worksite, or acting under the influence of alcohol while at the worksite, at an (organization) function, or in furtherance of organization business, is unacceptable employee conduct and is strictly prohibited.

Risk Management. (Organization) shall maintain a policy of risk management/loss control designed to correct problems and will provide on-the-job wellness programs and/or counseling or referrals whenever possible.

16

Conflicts of Interest

Discussion

The conduct of employees in activities other than within the organization can lead to conflicts of interest, with negative results for the employee, the organization, or both. Conflicts may also occur within the organization. The organization therefore should establish a policy regarding internal as well as external conflicts of interest.

Membership on Board

No staff member shall sit on the Board of (organization) where direct input concerning the governance of this organization would be possible.

Former staff members shall not serve on the Board of Directors for a minimum of one year from the time of their separation from (organization).

Board members of (organization) must resign from the board prior to submitting an application for employment.

Outside Employment

(Organization) discourages its full-time employees from taking employment outside of the organization. If an employee is planning to take an outside job, he or she must give notice in writing to the Executive Director, for inclusion in the employee's personnel file. In the case of the Executive Director, notice of outside employment should be given to the Personnel Chair of (organization).

Outside employment will not be considered an excuse for poor job performance, absenteeism, tardiness, leaving early, refusal to travel, or refusal to work overtime or different hours. The organization will not pay medical benefits for injuries or sickness resulting from employment at an outside organization.

17

Posting of Notices

Description

Organizations are required by various federal and state laws to post certain notices at the workplace. The state requirements vary, so state requirements should be checked in each case.

(Organization) shall post state and federal regulatory guidelines at a prominent location in the workplace. These shall include Industrial Welfare Commission's Orders, Payday Notices, On the Job Safety and Health Protection, Equal Employment Opportunity Statement, Notice of Compensation Carrier, Notice of EDD and SAIF Compliance, Notice of Time Off to Vote, Tobacco Warning, Minimum Wage and Overtime Statement, Occupational Safety and Health Act, and other notices as may be required by federal or state law.

18

Signature Page

Discussion

A signature page allows the organization to keep track of who has received and read the manual. It reiterates the disclaimer provisions regarding employment contracts and should be signed by each person who receives a manual.

I ACKNOWLEDGE THAT I HAVE READ AND UNDERSTAND THE POLICIES AND PROCEDURES MANUAL OF (ORGANIZATION) (HEREINAFTER THE "MANUAL").

THIS MANUAL, HOWEVER, IS NOT A CONTRACT OF EMPLOYMENT OR A GUARANTEE OF FUTURE EMPLOYMENT FOR ANY PARTICULAR PERIOD OF TIME AND SHOULD NOT BE CONSTRUED AS SUCH. IT IS UNDERSTOOD THAT EMPLOYMENT WITH (ORGANIZATION) IS DEEMED TO BE EMPLOYMENT AT WILL, WHEREBY EITHER THE EMPLOYEE OR THE ORGANIZATION HAS THE DISCRETION TO TERMINATE EMPLOYMENT OR TO TAKE ANY OTHER ACTION REGARDING EMPLOYMENT THAT IS IN ITS BEST INTERESTS. NO PERSON OTHER THAN THE BOARD OF DIRECTORS HAS ANY AUTHORITY TO MODIFY THIS POLICY OR TO ENTER INTO ANY WRITTEN AGREEMENT THAT IS CONTRARY TO THIS POLICY.

ANY QUESTIONS I HAVE ON THESE POLICIES HAVE BEEN ANSWERED SATISFACTORILY. I ALSO ACKNOWLEDGE THAT THE POLICIES CONTAINED IN THE MANUAL MAY BE AMENDED OR OMITTED AT ANY TIME. I WILL ACKNOWLEDGE CHANGES WITH MY SIGNATURE AND THE DATE SIGNED.

(Please sign and date this page and return it to
_____ within _____ days).

_____   _____

EMPLOYEE SIGNATURE   DATE

_____

DATE MANUAL PREPARED BY BOARD

_____

BOARD AUTHORIZED SIGNATURE

Appendix 1

Specific employment related questions and concerns (listed below) should be directed to the following federal agencies. The addresses for each of these agencies is listed in Appendix 2.

Afirmative Action contact the Equal Employment Opportunity Commission (EEOC)

Age Discrimination contact the Equal Employment Opportunity Commission (EEOC)

Child Labor Laws contact the Employment Standards Administration (ESA)

Disabilities Disrimination contact the Equal Employment Opportunity Commission (EEOC)

Disability Benefits contact the Social Security Administration (SSA)

Employee Benefit Plans contact the Pension Benefit Guaranty Corporation (PBCG)

Employee Discrimination contact the Equal Employment Opportunity Commission (EEOC)

Equal Pay contact the Equal Employment Opportunity Commission (EEOC)

Health Insurance contact the Justice Department (JD)

Life Insurance contact the Justice Department (JD)

Medicare contact the Social Security Administration (SSA)

Migrant and Foreign Workers contact the Employment Standards Administration (ESA)

Minimum Wage Law contact the Employment Standards Administration (ESA)

Occupational Safety and Health contact the Occupational Safety Health Administration (OSHA)

Social Security Benefits contact the Social Security Administration (SSA)

Unemployment Compensation contact the U.S. Department of Labor (Contact State Programs)

Workers Compensation contact the Justice Department (JD)

Appendix 2

Addresses and phone numbers of important federal agencies to contact with employment related questions.

1. Equal Employment Opportunity Comission (EEOC)
   1801 L Street, NW
   Washington, DC 20507
   1-800-669-EEOC/1-800-800-3302(TDD)

2. Employment Standards Administration (ESA)
   Office of Public Affairs
   200 Constitution Avenue, NW, Room C4331
   Washington, DC 20201
   202-523-8743

3. Justice Department
   10th Street Constitution Avenue, NW
   Washington, DC 20530
   202-514-2000

4. Department of Health and Human Services
   Social Security Administration
   PO Box 17739
   Baltimore, MD 21235
   1-800-772-1213

5. Pension and Welfare Benefits Administration
   200 Constitution Avenue, NW, Room 5658
   Washington, DC 20212
   1-202-523-8784

6. Communications and Public Affairs Department
   Pension Benefit Guaranty Corporation
   2020 K Street, NW
   Washington, DC 2000-1860
   1-202-778-8800

7. Office of Information and Consumer Affairs
   Department of Labor, OSHA
   200 Constitution Avenue, NW, Room N 3647
   Washington, DC 20210
   1-202-523-8148

Appendix 3

Personal File Entry Form

Opening Date: _____

Primary Data:

Name _____

Current Address _____

City _____ State _____ Zip _____

Home Phone _____

Date of Birth _____

Social Security No. _____

Contact in case of emergency:

Name _____

Phone _____

Historical Information

DATE FILED

Employment Verification_____

Resume _____

Application on File_____

Emergency Health Issues Alert _____

Entry Level Salary $ _____

Applicable Forms on File

(Must be updated at least annually)

DATE FILED

W-4 Withholding Allowance _____

State Withholding Form (if applicable) _____

Insurance Application or waiver_____

Sign-off on Personnel Policies _____

Sign-off on Emergency Preparedness Plan _____

Performance Appraisal Information

DATE FILED

Performance Evaluation(s) _____

Promotions/Salary Adjustments

$_____ (19   )

$_____ (19   )

Commendations (permanent)_____

Disciplinary Reports (annual) _____

Attendance Reports (Current and on File in

Appropriate Area) _____

Use additional sheets and include in file, as current and necessary.